# CHOOSING A BIBLE TRANSLATION

# Choosing a Bible Translation

John J. Pilch

**LITURGICAL PRESS**
Collegeville, Minnesota

www.litpress.org

Cover design by Nora Koch

ISBN 978-0-8146-2581-1

| | 2 | 3 | 4 | 5 | 6 | 7 | 8 |
|---|---|---|---|---|---|---|---|

**Library of Congress Cataloging-in-Publication Data**

Pilch, John J.
    Choosing a Bible translation / John J. Pilch.
        p.    cm.
    Includes bibliographical references.
    ISBN 0-8146-2581-9 (alk. paper)
    1. Bible—Versions, English.   2. Bible—Translating.  I. Title.

  BS455.P476   2000
  220.5'2—dc21

                          00-021136

When a person determines to read and study the Bible seriously, his or her first question usually is: "Which Bible translation is the best one to use or to buy?" The Bible at home may be quite old, perhaps even a family treasure. Many people who begin to read and study such a Bible soon discover that its language is "old fashioned" and the book itself is cumbersome to carry and clumsy to use. What, then, should one look for in a Bible to be used for study purposes?

## Two Kinds of Translations

In general, there are two kinds of Bible translations: a word-for-word (literal, or formal correspondence) translation and a meaning-for-meaning (literary, or dynamic equivalence) translation. A song popular many years ago poked fun at the word-for-word or literal translations familiar to anyone who struggled to learn French in high school: "The pen of my aunt is on the table of my uncle." If you knew French, you would have had no difficulty translating this clumsy English sentence back into perfect French.

Word-for-word (literal) Bible translations include the King James Version (1611) and its literary descendants: the American Standard Version (1901), the Revised Standard Version (1952), the New Revised Standard Version (1989); the New King James Version (1982); the New American Bible (1970) with Revised New Testament (1986) and Revised Psalms (1991); the New International Version (1983); and the New Jerusalem Bible (1985). Anyone who knows Hebrew, Aramaic, and Greek would be able to translate those English versions back into their original languages almost perfectly with relative ease.

Meaning-for-meaning (literary) translations produce a simplified text for easier reading. The major concern of this kind of translation is that the English text should produce in the reader the same effect as the original would. For example, the Polish language has one set of words for "aunt" and "uncle" on one's father's side *(stryjenka, stryj)* and a different set of words for "aunt" and "uncle" on one's mother's side *(wujenka* [or *ciotka*], *wuj).* The difference is so important as to require special renditions in translation. In English we would say "my paternal uncle" or "my maternal uncle," but that strikes us as affected or awkward. We prefer the simple words "aunt" and "uncle." The general meaning is clear, even if we decide to sacrifice the precision of the Polish language. The same would be true for translations of kinship vocabulary in the Hebrew Bible (see comments about TEV below).

Meaning-for-meaning Bible translations include the Jerusalem Bible (1966), the New English Bible (1970), Today's English Version also known as the Good News Bible (1976), the Revised English Bible (1989), and the Contemporary English Version (1996).

Generally speaking, the best kind of Bible for serious study is a word-for-word (literal) translation. A reader can clearly see what the original text seems to be saying, and the footnotes in study editions explain the difficulties. On the other hand, the best kind of Bible for reading, whether privately or in public, is a meaning-for-meaning or literary translation.

Since modern Bible translations are generally produced by teams of scholars rather than by one person, word-for-word versions differ among themselves and sometimes begin to look like meaning-for-meaning versions. In truth, neither of these two kinds of translations is "pure." Each has a mixture of both approaches. Yet even taking this into consideration, the distinction between the two general kinds of translations is still a useful one.

*Sample Text*

Make a list of some of your favorite passages and look them up whenever you examine a new translation. Notice how similar or different the translation is compared with others familiar to you. For example, in Gen 31:35 Rachel explains to Laban that she cannot rise from the saddle on which she is sitting *ki derek nashim li*. The Hebrew literally states "because the way of women is upon me." What does that mean in plain English? How would you translate it? Which translation do you prefer? Why is that your preference?

Or consider the well-known description of *agape* in 1 Cor 13:1-13. The literary form of this passage (a depersonalized form of "confession," that is, an impersonal presentation of desirable qualities) requires a listing of ten elements: "Love is patient, is kind, does not envy, does not boast, is not proud, is not rude, is not self-seeking, is not easily angered, keeps no record of wrongs, does not delight in evil but rejoices in truth" (New International Version). Each time you examine a new translation, compare the ten elements in this passage with the translation you like. Is the order different? Has the translator rendered the Greek words differently? Can you make sense out of the new translation? We will review other passages later when considering inclusive language and related translation challenges.

## Word for Word (literal, formal correspondence) Translations

*The Revised Standard Version (RSV)*

The Bible translation most often recommended for study purposes is the Revised Standard Version (RSV). It is very faithful to the original biblical languages, yet it combines accuracy and clarity with solemn formality and a certain adherence to traditional "Bible English." The King James Version (KJV) established "Bible English" which held uninterrupted sway in Christian piety and English literature and style for more than 250 years. The discovery of some new biblical manuscripts and the recognition that some of the "Bible English" was going stale prompted a revision of the King James Version between 1881 and 1885. That revision became known as the English Revised Version. American scholars adapted this version for American readers and produced the American Standard Version in 1901.

Hardly was the American Standard Version completed when a committee was set up to determine whether further revisions would be needed. Their deliberations resulted in the production of the Revised Standard Version in 1952, a translation intended for both public worship and private study and reading. It eliminated "thees" and "thous" and changed some three hundred English words that in King James's day had quite a different meaning than they do today. For example, in the King James Version "wealth" really means "well-being," and "demand" simply means "ask." Yet the Revised Standard Version's concern for "Bible English" permitted the retention of "lo," "behold," and "yea."

Over the years the Revised Standard Version has gained and still retains immense respect. It is still used in many seminaries and universities and wherever the Bible is seriously studied because it is remarkably (though not always) consistent in its formal correspondence (literal) approach. The late Richard Cardinal Cushing of Boston granted an *imprimatur* to the 1965 edition of the Revised Standard Version published as the Oxford Annotated Bible with the Apocrypha, which included notes for the benefit of Catholic readers.

In 1971, a second edition of the RSV New Testament was published. In 1973 the New Oxford Annotated Bible with the Apocrypha—An Ecumenical Study Bible enhanced the Revised Standard Version still more with improved introductions, annotations, maps reflecting recent archaeological discoveries, and supplementary articles, including one on modern approaches to Bible study authored by the Roman Catholic scholar Fr. Roland E. Murphy, O.Carm.

The 1977 edition did away with the need for "Protestant" and "Catholic" editions of the Revised Standard Version by including "all the books accepted as authoritative by all the branches of the Christian Church" (Protestant, Anglican, Roman Catholic, and Eastern Orthodox).

## The New Revised Standard Version (NRSV)

Begun in 1974, this revision of the entire RSV was completed and published in 1991. The translators of the NRSV were mandated to introduce the changes required by concerns for improved accuracy, clarity, euphony, and current English-language usage. The guiding principle was: "As literal as possible, as free as necessary." The translators also sought to be as inclusive as possible both by presenting a complete range of biblical books from different canons as well as demonstrating sensitivity to gender inclusivity in translation. This latter is achieved by introducing plural forms when this does not distort the meaning of the passage.

This translation was intended for public reading and congregational worship, private study, Bible instruction, and meditation. Within a short while, four study Bibles were published based on the NRSV: the New Oxford Annotated Bible (1991), the NRSV Harper Study Bible (1991), the HarperCollins Study Bible (1993), and the Cambridge Annotated Study Bible (1993). Catholic scholars served on the committees that prepared each of these editions. Of the four, the HarperCollins is probably the most nearly complete and up-to-date for study purposes.

## The New American Bible (NAB)

The first English translation of the New Testament by Roman Catholics was published at Rheims, France, in 1582; the Old Testament was published at Douay in 1609. This version translated from the Vulgate (Latin Bible) is known as the Douay-Rheims Bible. Between 1749 and 1772 the

Douay-Rheims Bible underwent revision by Bishop Challoner, vicar-apostolic of London. The Douay-Rheims-Challoner translation was the authoritative Bible in use among English-speaking Roman Catholics until recent times. This translation from the Latin earned its position chiefly because Latin was the language of Roman Catholic worship and theological study. St. Jerome made this translation from Hebrew and Greek into Latin. Throughout the centuries when Latin was widely understood by elites, practically everyone concerned could hear the Scripture in a "common" language. This is why Jerome's Latin translation was known as the Vulgate, an adjective from the verb meaning "to make common, to make generally accessible."

In his encyclical *Divino Afflante Spiritu* (1943), Pope Pius XII encouraged Catholic scholars to produce Bible translations from the original languages. The American bishops then invited the members of the Catholic Biblical Association of America to translate the Hebrew, Aramaic, and Greek texts afresh. The resulting work by some fifty biblical scholars was published in 1970 as the New American Bible. This translation is clear, straightforward, scholarly, generally reliable, and pays careful attention to early manuscripts discovered at Qumran (1947 and later, often referred to as the Dead Sea Scrolls) and Masada, especially when these earlier texts shed light on the later Hebrew or Greek texts. The Hebrew manuscripts at Qumran, for instance, date from the first century A.D. Until their discovery in 1947, the earliest Hebrew manuscripts we possessed dated from the ninth century A.D.

While the New American Bible served well for serious study as well as private reading, experience was demonstrating that it had not been entirely satisfactory for public worship. Therefore a revision of the New Testament was published in 1987. Special attention was given to the question of discriminatory language, particularly with regard to language that sounded to modern ears as anti-Semitic and language that appeared to discriminate against minorities. Efforts were made to incorporate inclusive language in passages directed to men and women alike. A revision of the Psalms was published in 1991 reflecting the increased interest in inclusive translations. The entire Old Testament translation is currently being revised.

The Catholic Study Bible edited by Fr. Donald Senior, C.P., was based on the NAB and published in 1990 including the revised New Testament, articles, and other aids for studying the Bible.

## New International Version (NIV)

In 1966 a group of scholars representing many different denominations, including Anglican, Assemblies of God, Baptist, Brethren, Christian Reformed, Church of Christ, Evangelical Free, Lutheran, Mennonite, Methodist, Nazarene, Presbyterian, Wesleyan, and others, began a translation that they hoped by their collaborative efforts would truly earn the name "International." The New Testament was completed in 1973 and was distributed free on college campuses. The complete Bible was published in 1978 after at least three complete revisions; it was completely revised again for publication in 1983.

The translators sought accuracy, clarity, and literary quality in order to produce a translation suitable for public and private reading, teaching, preaching, memorizing, and liturgical use. They also sought continuity with tradition. This version claims to be more than a word-for-word translation, yet it does not stray very far from that model. Though Paulist Press published an ecumenical study edition of the New Testament in 1986, the translation is regarded by scholars as reflecting the Evangelical commitment of those involved in preparing it. All serious students of the Bible would benefit from comparing this translation with any of the others mentioned. Such a comparison will help to highlight difficult choices in variant readings and also help to understand how scholars determine which reading to place in the text and which in the footnote as an alternative reading.

To summarize, the best Bible translation for purposes of serious study is one that is concerned about literal fidelity to the original languages. That kind of translation is known technically as a "formal correspondence" or "linguistic equivalence" translation. In simpler terms, it is a word-for-word, or literal, translation. The RSV, NRSV, NAB, and NIV represent that kind of translation. The value of each as a study Bible is especially enhanced in the editions that provide commentary, notes, and study guides.

## Meaning for Meaning (literary, dynamic equivalence) Translations

*Jerusalem Bible (JB) and the New Jerusalem Bible (NJB)*

One of the first and richest fruits of Catholic scholarship after Pope Pius XII's encyclical *Divino Afflante Spiritu* was the French translation of the Bible from the original languages, with up-to-date critical introductions and notes, produced in fascicle form between 1948 and 1954 by the Dominicans at the École Biblique in Jerusalem (hence its title: *La Bible de Jérusalem*). The fascicles were gathered into a one-volume edition in 1956, and another completely revised one-volume edition was published in 1973. Its excellent translation, introductions, footnotes, and cross-references made this French language book a superb study Bible. A new edition was published in 1998.

An English translation of the 1956 French volume, called the Jerusalem Bible (JB), was published in 1966 under the editorship of the British biblical scholar Rev. Alexander Jones to mixed critical reviews. In 1985 Fr. Henry Wansbrough, O.S.B., edited a fresh English translation based on the 1973 French volume. This revised edition is called the New Jerusalem Bible.

Anyone comparing the New Jerusalem Bible with its predecessor will immediately see the improvements. The introductions and footnotes are quite obviously different and have been updated with scholarly insights gained since 1973. In the biblical text itself, paraphrase has been more rigorously avoided, and a commendable effort to avoid the inbuilt sexism of the English language has greatly improved the translation. Even so, it has retained the impressive poetic character of the 1966 English translation.

It still seems to fit well in the mouth, testifying to the lasting influence of the first collaborators that included such literary giants as J.R.R. Tolkien, Walter Shewring, Robert Speaight, and announcers of the British Broadcasting Corporation. Like its predecessor (JB), the New Jerusalem Bible is likely to be a first choice for public reading in drama or in worship.

## *Revised English Bible (REB)*

The translation chain extending from the King James Version to the American Standard Version and on to the Revised Standard Version consistently favored "Bible English." This led the Church of Scotland to invite other interested Churches to join in sponsoring a translation in a more contemporary English idiom. A committee of three eminent biblical scholars—C. H. Dodd, Godfrey Driver, and W. D. McHardy—supervised the work, which was finally published in 1970 as the New English Bible with the Apocrypha.

The New Testament, which was first published in 1962, appeared in the 1970 edition with almost three hundred alterations in response to suggestions for improvement. In 1976 Oxford University Press published the New English Bible with the Apocrypha-Oxford Study Edition, edited by the Jewish scholar Samuel Sandmel, the Christian scholar M. J. Suggs, and the Catholic scholar A. J. Tkacik. With the added introduction, annotations, and cross-references, as well as other study tools, this edition was a marked improvement over the plain translation of 1970.

In general, this translation gives priority to spoken (or heard) language over the written language and to the needs of the audience over the forms of the language. Nevertheless, inclusion of the nonsense word "Jehovah" (the combination of the consonants of the Hebrew word in the biblical text "YaHWeH" with the vowels of the Hebrew word actually spoken "Adonai") was puzzling.

In 1989, a substantial revision of the New English Bible under the direction of McHardy was published with the Apocrypha as the Revised English Bible. The revisers dropped "Jehovah," abandoned the "thou" form in prayers, and judiciously used gender-inclusive language in passages that undoubtedly apply to both genders. They increased the number of textual sub-headings that are printed in italic type and included a table of measures, weights, and values.

### Good News Bible (Today's English Version, TEV)

The American Bible Society has a long history of dedication to disseminating the Bible all over the world in easily understandable translations based on solid scholarly research. After it published the New Testament in Today's English Version (Good News for Modern Man) in 1966, the American Bible Society set itself to translating the Old Testament as well. In 1976 the completed project, the Good News Bible (Today's English Version), was offered to the public.

The language of this translation is natural, clear, simple, and unambiguous, since it was intended for people everywhere for whom English is either the native or acquired tongue. The goal was to produce a faithful translation of the *meaning* of the Hebrew, Aramaic, and Greek texts. There was no attempt to reproduce in English the parts of speech, sentence structure, word order, and grammatical devices of the original languages.

Moreover, the translation has rendered variations on names in the Hebrew text with a single name in the English, just as the New International Version does. For instance, in the Hebrew text Moses' father-in-law is called Reuel in Exod 2:18 and Jethro in Exod 3:1. The difference in names is one of the many clues that help a reader separate the Elohist tradition (Exod 3:1) from the Yahwist tradition (Exod 2:18). But the Good News Bible uses the name Jethro everywhere, no matter what the Hebrew text says. This is an example of a meaning-for-meaning translation (namely, the father-in-law) in contrast to a word-for-word translation (namely, the different names assigned to a single person by different traditions).

Such a tendency toward commentary and paraphrase in the Good News Bible marks it as a highly successful example of a meaning-for-meaning translation but makes it less suitable for a serious study of the text. A reader interested in following the advice of the Vatican Council II to focus on literary forms or other literary devices as a key to grasping the meaning of biblical texts would be impeded (see the Dogmatic Constitution on Divine Revelation, no. 12).

In 1985 the New Catholic Study Bible—St. Jerome Edition, utilizing the text of the Good News Bible as its base, was published. It contains valuable articles and useful introductions, but the decision to print Jesus' words in red ink is lamentable. That printing custom tends to encourage the erroneous belief that the Evangelists were present on the spot and recorded literally everything Jesus said like faithful stenographers. To resurrect such a custom today in a study Bible is a disservice unless the significance of the color is fully spelled out. Historically, this practice originated in 1852 to indicate the words spoken by Jesus during his lifetime in contrast to those spoken by him in visions. Eventually that distinction disappeared, hence the need to explain the color more clearly wherever it appears in modern editions.

Finally, if readers are expected to "study" this Bible and to learn how to use it, then listing the page numbers of biblical references in the Biblical Cyclopedic Index would seem to defeat that very purpose. Nearly all modern readers of the Bible need to learn how to find books of the Bible by their more or less traditional locations since page numbers differ from translation to translation and edition to edition.

## Contemporary English Version (CEV)

Originally intended as a translation for children ages five to nine, the CEV (begun in 1985) was so appealing to adults that the translators (the American Bible Society) decided to direct the translation to this wider readership. Thus it was translated especially for the listener, yet also for the reader and for those unfamiliar with traditional biblical language. The translators wanted it to be "user-friendly" so that it could be "read aloud without stumbling, heard without misunderstanding, and listened to with enjoyment and appreciation because the language is contemporary and the style is lucid and lyrical."

This translation attempts to make Scripture easily understandable to the modern listener and less subject to misinterpretation. When Paul refers to a form of physical punishment he received by saying "once I was stoned" (2 Cor 11:25), in modern ears that phrase relates to drug abuse and unfailingly causes the listener to snicker or laugh. Hence the CEV translates: "once my enemies stoned me." Still, this lively, fresh, and readable translation had to sacrifice some of the exegetical sensitivity that distinguished the Good News Bible. Too often discourse links are omitted, thus forcing the reader to guess at the meaning intended by the sacred author.

The CEV New Testament and Psalms have received the *imprimatur*. Catholics may use it with confidence. The *Lectionary for Masses with Children* which received approval from Rome draws its readings from the CEV. In general, though, while this translation eliminates the need for explanations when people first begin to read the Bible, a more literal translation would be preferable for serious intellectual study of the Bible.

To summarize, meaning-for-meaning translations strive for effect, especially in public reading. As a result, accuracy of translation and fidelity to the text are sometimes sacrificed. The New Jerusalem Bible, the Revised English Bible, the Good News Bible, and the Contemporary English Version all lean—to a lesser or greater degree—in the direction of meaning-for-meaning translations. This factor makes them less useful as study Bibles, although good footnotes, introductions, and other annotations often compensate. Yet some critics would even question the utility of this kind of translation for worship. While the idea of a stirring reading is highly desirable, these critics wonder at what point the word of God, which is sharper than a two-edged sword, needs to be replaced by the literary cleverness of a paraphraser's words.

There is no "official" or privileged English translation of the Bible. The Catholic Bishops of the United States and the United Kingdom each have commissioned and approved English translations for their respective countries. At the same time, other English translations have also been approved particularly in special study editions featuring background articles and other information helpful to the reader. The Church urges that translations should be based on the best manuscripts available and reflect the best scholarship known. Catholics are free to choose whichever Bible meets these criteria and suits their specific interests and purposes.

In general, it remains true that the best translation for purposes of serious study is a word-for-word translation and the best translation for pleasurable reading privately or in public is a meaning-for-meaning translation. Some Bible students might be interested in comparing both to discover the differences and decide the relative advantages and disadvantages of each translation. In 1996, Oxford University Press published *The Complete Parallel Bible* which addresses this concern directly. It contains the Old and New Testaments with the apocryphal and deuterocanonical books and presents four translations in parallel columns: NRSV (literal, United States), REB (literary, Great Britain), NAB (literal, United States), and NJB (literary, Great Britain). The NRSV, NAB, and NJB have *imprimaturs;* the REB is approved for use by Catholics in Great Britain. The Bible is intended for use by Protestant, Anglican, Roman Catholic, and Orthodox Christian communities. The order follows that of the NRSV. In order to keep this Bible to a reasonable size, notes were kept to a minimum. For more complete information, the reader is advised to consult the NAB. The book is affordable and relatively easy to use. Yet computer-literate Bible readers will immediately wonder whether this kind of comparative study might be accomplished more quickly and easily with software. The answer, of course, is yes.

### Bibles on Computer Software

It is now possible not only to obtain electronic copies of individual English translations of the Bible but also CDs which bundle more than one translation together with a host of resources (e.g., maps, commentaries, etc.). The *Liguori Bible Library* contains three approved translations: NAB, NRSV Catholic Edition; RSV with Apocrypha, and includes Barclay's popular and widely used *Daily Study Bible Series: New Testament*, Greek and Hebrew Definitions, and Nave's Topic Index. The *Logos Catholic Collection* (http:// www.logos.com/products/catholiccollection) offers the NAB, NJB, the Latin Vulgate, the Jerome Biblical Commentary, and the *Confessions* of St. Augustine, with the option of adding other resources.

One of the most extensive collections of translations and other sources (directed primarily to scholars but certainly of interest to serious Bible students) is *Bible Works 4* (http://www.bibleworks.com), which features fifty-eight Bible translations in twenty languages along with other resources. The English versions are KJV, NKJV, NASB, NASB 1995, RSV with Apocrypha, NIV, NRSV with Apocrypha, Webster's, ASV 1901, Young's Literal Translation, Darby, Bible in Basic English, NAB, Douai-Rheims 1899 American Edition, New Living Translation, and the New Jerusalem Bible.

A good resource for Bible translations and other resources available on the Internet can be found at http://www.mcgill.ca/religion/link-bib.htm. A hard-copy resource, *High Places in Cyberspace: A Guide to Biblical and Religious Studies, Classics, and Archaeological Resources on the Internet* by Patrick Durusau (Atlanta: Scholars Press, 1998) promises updates at http://scholarspress.org/scripts/highplaces.html. This book lists well-screened and critically evaluated sites.

## Special Challenges

*Inclusive Language*

More recent translations like the NRSV have sought to eliminate "linguistic sexism arising from the inherent bias of the English language toward the masculine gender" (Introduction by Bruce Metzger, General Editor). This bias is considered to have restricted or obscured the meaning of the original text. Thus the translators sought to eliminate masculine forms appearing in obvious references to men and women "without altering passages that reflect the historical situation of ancient patriarchal culture."

This effort was not always successful. In fact in some instances it did not fairly represent the culture. In the ancient Mediterranean world, boys and girls were raised together by all the women without significant presence of men. Boys were pampered and pleasured. They were breast-fed twice as long as girls (see 2 Macc 7:27; see 1 Sam 1:22-25). When at the age of puberty boys were pushed without the benefit of a rite of passage (bar-mitzvah is Talmudic in origin) into the harsh men's world, adult men had to teach them how to behave like a man. Proverbs (13:24; 19:18; 22:15; 23:13-14; 29:15, 17) and Sir 30:1-13 indicate that the means of instruction was harsh physical discipline. Young girls never were and still aren't reared in this fashion in the Mediterranean world.

The Hebrew words in Proverbs are *son* (13:24; 19:18; 29:17) and *lad* (22:15; 23:13-14; 29:15). Except for 22:15 where it translates the word as "boy," thus correctly reflecting the gender, the NRSV renders the other Hebrew masculine nouns in the plural: "children." This is not only incorrect but culturally implausible. Girls simply are not physically disciplined by their fathers. The "inclusive" translation of these Proverbs transfers the fusion of love and violence so patent in the treatment of boys in Mediterranean culture (see Sir 30:1) to Mediterranean girls as well. When adopted by Western readers who tend to use the Bible as a warrant for behavior, the inclusive translation of these verses permits the unfortunate transfer of a Mediterranean cultural value into Western culture where it is not acceptable but punishable by arrest, fine, or imprisonment.

The author of Hebrews confirms these observations in his reflections on Jesus. While he was on earth, Jesus offered up prayers and supplications (see e.g., Mark 14:34-36) to his father to take the cup away. But *"precisely because* he was Son, he learned obedience through what he suffered" (Heb 5:8), just as Proverbs teaches. The translation "because" in Heb 5:8 is preferable to "although." In the sacred author's mind, the way the Father treated Jesus is not an exception to the culture (although) but rather quite appropriate (precisely because). A little later that author quotes Prov 3:11-12 (the Lord disciplines those whom he loves, once again reflecting Mediterranean culture's customary fusion of love and violence) and then says, literally, God is treating you as a father treats sons. The NRSV renders this passage with plurals (Proverbs replaces "son" with "children"; and Heb 12:7 replaces "son" with "children"), once again unwittingly misrepresenting ancient Mediterranean culture and offering dangerous and erroneous suggestions to modern Western readers.

The issue of gender inclusive language, quite peculiar to the English language and the Western world, is indeed a serious and important consideration. The Bible, however, originated in the non-Western world whose languages reflect the fundamental gender-based division of all of reality and life. Balancing these two realities, namely one culture's preference for gender-based division with another culture's preference for gender inclusivity, is not an easy task. Considerate readers may have to learn increased tolerance for ancient peoples who are culturally different from them just as they remain equally challenged to appreciate cultural diversity in their own world. Bible readers are concerned above all with learning the honest truth about the people who populate the pages of the Bible. Respect for their culture is a good starting point.

## Social System

The Hebrew language has at least two words that are translated "virgin." The word in Isa 7:14 *(alma)* actually means maiden, a woman of marriageable and child-bearing age. In this instance the reference is very likely to the king's wife, already pregnant with a male heir who will assure the continuation of the Davidic line. In Gen 24:16, Rebekah is described as a virgin *(betulah),* and as often happens in the Bible, a phrase in apposition clarifies: "whom no man had known." Scholars recognize that the dictionary alone will not help in translating these words since they are not used with the precision that modern readers expect. Cultural context, however, is not only helpful but necessary.

*Textual Variants*

We possess hundreds of manuscripts which differ significantly among themselves. Scholars have gathered them, organized and evaluated their reliability and trustworthiness, and developed well honed guidelines and principles for deciding which manuscripts might contain the more plausibly original version. This alone, however, can prove inadequate.

In John 7:8, Jesus says he is "not going up to this feast" but in v. 10 he does go. Some ancient manuscripts, indeed the best, have "not *yet* going up to this feast." On the basis of manuscript evidence itself, deciding which of these two translations should be preferred is a very close call. The NIV reports in its text "not yet going up to this feast" very likely on the basis of the evidence which holds a slight edge. But the judgment might also be made on the basis of the translator's avowed commitment to the "authority and infallibility of the bible as God's word in written form." The translators believe that the Bible contains divine answers to the deepest needs of humanity. Humankind's need for truthfulness and honesty is certainly basic.

Indeed to choose the other reading (not going up, but then he goes up) runs the risk of making it seem that Jesus lies. The scholarly principle that guides the decision to place this in the text and its alternative in a footnote is the value of selecting the "harder reading," that is, the one that may be embarrassing or seem incongruous. In other words, which is more likely? That the original report was consistent but a later hand added what seems like a lie? Or that the original report contained an apparent deception but a later hand removed it as unbecoming to Jesus? Most translations do indeed place this harder reading in the text and the alternative in the footnote. Yet, while the reading is "harder" to the Western reader, it is quite normal to the Mediterranean reader whose culture views secrecy, deception, and lying as legitimate strategies for preserving one's honor and defending one's life, as Jesus is doing in this situation. In other words, this version is culturally more plausible than the "consistent" readings preferred by other translations.

## *Lack of Cultural Awareness*

For a final example, consider the phrase "evil eye" that occurs in both the Hebrew Bible and the Greek New Testament. It is very rarely translated literally, though sometimes it is reported in the footnote. The customary translation is envy, miserliness, hatred, greed, covetousness, and the like. The texts include Deut 15:7-11; 28:53-57; Prov 14:8; 23:6; 28:22; Sir 14:3, 6, 8, 10; 18:18; 31:13; 37:11; Tobit 4:7, 16; Wis 4:10, 12; and in the New Testament: Matt 6:22-23//Luke 11:34-36; Matt 20:1-15; Mark 7:22; Gal 3:1.

In this culture where all goods are considered to be finite in quantity and already distributed, no one ever tries to get ahead. Those who seem to possess "more" than others are frequently objects of the "evil eye" (translated "greed"). The idea is: I like what you have but don't have it myself. I wish I could have it, but since I can't, I wish yours to be destroyed. This is considerably different from the notion of "envying" in the Western sense, where the envious person ultimately goes out and purchases something bigger, better, or more beautiful. I know of no translation that reports any of this understanding in its translation (rendering the Hebrew and Greek literally) or in its notes. It is, for instance, very plausible that the twelve-year-old girl whom Jesus raised from the dead (Mark 6:35-43) died as a result of the "evil eye" cast upon her (envy) by other parents who had lost children in a culture where infant mortality was quite high.

The point of these examples illustrating "special challenges" to translators is that the reader must remember that no translation is perfect. Translations will continue to proliferate at an even greater rate than at present because scholars are becoming increasingly aware of and informed about the Mediterranean culture which gives meaning to the Hebrew, Aramaic, and Greek (and other) languages.

# Conclusion

The British biblical scholar C. S. Rodd observed that at the present time we no longer have Protestant (KJV, NEB) and Catholic Bibles (Douay-Rheims, JB), but instead conservative Evangelical (NIV), academic (RSV/NRSV), and popular (GNB) ones. Indeed, scholarly consensus across denominations has replaced doctrinal intransigence in translation. Rodd's observation appears to be quite on target. The enterprise of translating Bibles has improved enormously in this century, especially in the second half, but it still has far to go.

In deciding which Bible is the best to use for purposes of study, one ought perhaps to follow the academic route even if one is not enrolled in a seminary or university program. The academic route is that of the literal, word-for-word, formal correspondence translation. Yet as we have seen even these translations are frequently unaware of the Mediterranean cultural perspective which has not yet had sufficient impact upon scholars and others involved in the translations. The astute Bible student will always remember the Italian proverb: "Every translator is a traitor" *(Traduttore traditore)*. Of course, this does not mean the translator is devious. Rather the point is that translation is a difficult task. Even the best trained human beings sometimes fail to translate well, for many understandable reasons. Still, a Hebrew-less and Greek-less Bible student can learn how to evaluate translations critically by comparing many. Knowing how to distinguish between word-for-word and meaning-for-meaning translations is a giant first step in the right direction.